THE OFFICIAL RANGERS ANNUAL 2005

Written by
Douglas Russell

g

A Grange Publication

© 2004. Published by Grange Communications Ltd., Edinburgh, under licence from Rangers Football Club. Printed in the EU.

ISBN 1-902704-75-4

£6.99

CONTENTS

THE MANAGER

ALEX McLEISH

Manager Alex McLeish, now in his fourth season at the club after arriving as team manager in December 2001, was as disappointed as any true-blue following the events of Season 2003/04. After the Scottish Cup defeat at Celtic Park in early March, he was quoted as saying: 'When I came to Ibrox we wanted to sort things out in the first six months and I don't think there was any expectation that we would win one trophy never mind two. However, things were put to the side because of the pressure for success. Now there is a chance for Rangers to build for the next four or five years and I want to deliver......I want to be able to say I put my own stamp on my team and that I have left a youth infrastructure to be proud of. We are well on our way to achieving that and I believe we can also deliver a winning team on the field.' Earlier last season, Alex McLeish signed a long-term deal that will keep him at Rangers until 2007.

THE PLAYERS

STEFAN KLOS

Rangers fans were given a most welcome late Christmas present in January 2004 when it was confirmed that goalkeeper Stefan Klos, at the age of thirty-two, had signed a contract extension that will keep him at Ibrox until year 2007. Now on a par with the legendary Andy Goram, the German stopper was a shining light last season and performed at the highest level week in, week out for the whole of that 2003/04 period, fully justifying his Rangers Player of the Year award. Also the proud owner of a Champions League medal from his days with Borussia Dortmund, Klos was only twenty when he became their No 1 and was, for some years, the youngest regular Bundesliga goalkeeper in his homeland. It was, of course, Dick Advocaat, back in December 1998, who brought the player to Scotland and, two days after signing for the club on Christmas Eve, he made his Scottish debut in a league game with St. Johnstone at Ibrox. By the end of that season, Klos and legendary status were already walking hand in hand. Appointed Club Captain for season 2004/05.

MAURICE ROSS

With his commitment to Rangers never in doubt, the young Scot started in the club's first two outings last season - the SPL game against Kilmarnock at Ibrox (4-0, 9.8.03) and the Champions League qualifier with FC Copenhagen four days later that ended all-square at 1-1. His next two starts were in the impressive away and home league victories over Hearts (4-0, 21.9.03) and Dundee (3-1, 27.9.03) respectively. Although the player only started occasionally last term, Ross scored his first-ever Ibrox Rangers goal in the 4-0 early May victory over Motherwell after coming on as a second-half substitute for Alan Hutton. The full back was in the starting eleven at East End Park on the last day of the SPL season when Rangers, recording their first victory on the artificial surface, defeated Dunfermline 3-2.

ALAN HUTTON

After making his first-team debut against Partick Thistle at Firhill back in December 2002, the full-back made his first appearance last season when Dundee were comprehensively beaten 4-0 at Ibrox in late March. In a performance that certainly belied his youth, Hutton's tremendously assured play earned the youngster (a teenager until November 2004) a well deserved man-of-the-match award from the club sponsors. Three days later, in the re-arranged SPL clash with Dunfermline, his first-ever Ibrox goal gave Rangers an early lead in a game that finished 4-1 in favour of the home side. Although the week ended with defeat at the hands of Celtic, his Old Firm display that Sunday lunchtime offered all follow-followers great encouragement for the future. At that time, it was confirmed that Alan had signed a new deal with Rangers, keeping him at the club until 2007. In the mid-April league clash with Partick Thistle at Ibrox, the youngster turned provider and created the chances for both Rangers goals (converted by Steven Thompson and Gavin Rae) in the 2-0 victory. Hutton was then an ever-present for the remaining games of Season 2003/04.

FERNANDO RICKSEN

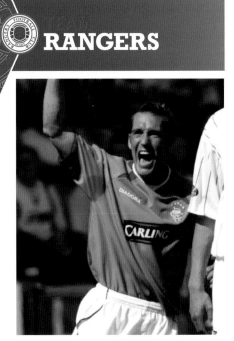

Rarely out of the news, Fernando Ricksen, who never gives less that 100% for the cause, started last season in a rich vein of form and was quietly impressive before a sickening clash of heads with team-mate Henning Berg (in the first half of the Champions League victory over Stuttgart at Ibrox) left him with a bad facial cut that required several stitches. Although under an entirely different set of circumstances, the Dutch international could have been injured even earlier in the season when, during the second game of the league campaign, a hooligan ran onto the pitch and tried to attack him before being grounded by local police officers. One month after the Stuttgart incident, he was, thankfully, back on duty for the clash with Motherwell at Fir Park. His only goal in the 2003/04 period (a superb right-foot rocket into the top corner) was on the last day of the season when 10-man Rangers came from behind to beat Dunfermline 3-2 at East End Park. Only two players (Stefan Klos and Michael Ball) started more league games for the club last term.

MICHAEL BALL

Following his terrible injury problems since arriving from the English Premiership, it was a genuine delight to see ex-Everton defender Michael

Ball line up with the rest of the Rangers team right at the very start of the 2003/04 campaign. Some four months later in the SPL encounter with Dundee at Dens Park, he scored the crucial second goal (a free-kick from forty yards out that sailed over everyone and into the net) on the day that Rangers recorded an important 2-0 win. The man with the tremendous left foot made more appearances for Rangers throughout the 2003/04 period than any other outfield player, with only goalkeeper Stefan Klos beating his grand total of 41 starts.

PAOLI VANOLI

The Italian left-sided defender scored one of THE goals of last season when, after appearing as substitute for Peter Lovenkrands in the home game with Dundee, he hit the most perfect thirty-five yard angled strike that screamed past a stunned Speroni in the visitors' goal. Prior to this, with the score level at 1-1, it looked as if Jim Duffy's outfit would take something from the late September clash. Towards the end of last season, Vanoli cemented his place in the team and started in six of the final eight SPL clashes. As manager Alex McLeish said after the dust had settled on the 2003/04 league campaign, 'Paoli Vanoli has done well. He has never given me a minute's problem and I felt he finished the season strongly – which I hope augurs well for next term.'

JEAN-ALAIN BOUMSONG

One of the most applauded young talents in European football, the strapping 6ft 3in Cameroon-born French central defender arrived at Ibrox on a five year deal in the summer of 2004. He had joined his previous club, Auxerre, after spending two seasons with First Division outfit Le Havre where he also attended university and gained a degree in mathematics. Following France's poor showing during the last World Cup tournament in Japan and South Korea, manager Jacques Santini brought Boumsong (the sixth Frenchman to have signed for Rangers) into the national squad where he is now seen, in many quarters, as a natural successor to the legendary Marcel Desailly in the team. The commanding stopper scored his first goal for France in the Euro 2004 qualifier against Israel in October 2003 and was then part of their 23-man squad for the summer finals of the same tournament in Portugal.

STRIKING GOLD

Top class strikers are a rare breed indeed and certainly worth their weight in gold. Over the years, many truly great goalscorers have worn the blue of Rangers and gone on to earn their place in the hearts of the fans. We have taken a brief look at four careers - from four different eras - and their exceptional exploits on the field of play and featured them throughout this year's Rangers Annual.

BOB McPHAIL

One of the most impressive exhibits in the Ibrox Trophy Room is a small cabinet which contains the finest collection of medals to be found in Scotland. Thirty-six in total (including seven for the Scottish Cup), they were all won by Bob McPhail from the days when legendary manager Bill Struth decreed that a Rangers player would always arrive at any away ground wearing blue overcoat with velvet collar, blue suit, white shirt and, of course, black shoes/socks.

McPhail joined from Airdrie in 1927 (for the princely sum of £4,500) after having netted 74 goals for the Lanarkshire outfit. It was with Airdrie, in fact, that he won the first of his Scottish Cup medals when they defeated Hibernian 2-0 in 1924 to lift the trophy for the only time in their history. Indeed, this was the last Scottish Cup Final to be held at Ibrox until Kilmarnock and Falkirk headed there in the summer of 1997 due to the unavailability of Hampden.

At Rangers, he formed a deadly left-wing partnership with the original 'Wee Blue Devil' Alan Morton and, at the end of his first season (1927/28), McPhail was second top scorer in the league (with seventeen goals) as a double of Championship and Scottish Cup was being celebrated at Ibrox for the very first time. In April, the Light Blues had ended their Scottish Cup hoodoo by lifting the trophy for the first time in twenty-five years following the famous 4-0 triumph over Celtic. In addition to scoring Rangers second goal that day, nobody bettered his six tournament strikes in that season's competition.

Indeed the Scottish Cup was good for him and Bob duly scored in the finals of 1932 (Rangers 3 Kilmarnock 0), 1934 (Rangers 5 St. Mirren 0) and 1936

Top class strikers are
a rare breed and certainly
worth their weight
in Gold!

(Rangers 1 Third Lanark 0) as well as also winning medals in both 1930 and 1935 although he failed to find the net on those last two Hampden occasions. Additionally, 'Greetin Boab' claimed a total of 106 goals in the five championship campaigns (1928/29 to 1932/33) which followed his first Ibrox season before eventually hitting a grand total of 230 in all league matches for the club.

And the story behind the 'Greetin Boab' nickname? Seemingly he barracked team-mate Torry Gillick during a game suggesting that maybe the player might just want to get on with the game instead of being too concerned about an injury! The name stuck.

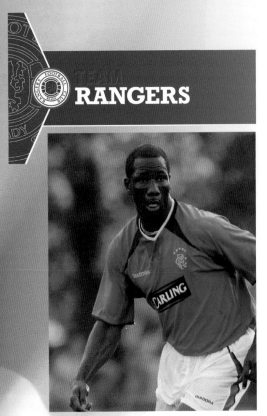

MARVIN ANDREWS

The giant ex-Livingston central defender, who previously rejected a move to Dundee United, arrived at the club on a two year agreement in the summer of 2004 after another impressive SPL season with the CIS Cup-winning West Lothian outfit. Andrews, a devout Christian, possesses an awesome physical presence and therefore brings a steely dimension to the Rangers back line of defence. At the end of May 2004, he played for his country in his adopted homeland when Scotland met Trinidad and Tobago on the football park for the very first time.

ZURAB KHIZANISHVILI

After joining Rangers from Dundee in the summer of 2003, the cultured Georgian made his different shade of blue debut in the opening SPL game of the season and immediately impressed all friends of Rangers. Right from the beginning, Khizanishvili was a revelation and only failed to start three matches before damaging a shoulder in the Champions League encounter with Panathinaikos at Ibrox in December. This injury would keep him sidelined for four weeks and meant that he was not available for the crucial championship clash with Celtic in the east end of Glasgow the following month. After returning to the starting line-up for four games, Zurab missed several other games before returning for the visit of Dundee to Ibrox in late March. After that, until the end of the season, he played in every game bar one.

BOB MALCOLM

Having been at the club since leaving school at 16, the versatile Malcolm partnered Zurab Khizanishvili at the centre of defence when Dundee United were beaten 3-1 at Tannadice in late August before continuing the relationship with the Georgian for the CIS Cup game with St. Johnstone at Ibrox. The score that night was 3-0 in favour of Rangers. Bob filled this central position again in the Glasgow encounter with Hearts (2-1, 20.12.03) but this time he was partnered by Henning Berg. The player signed a contract extension in January 2004 which will keep him at Ibrox until the summer of 2005. Malcolm unfortunately missed the latter stages of Season 2003/04 after being injured during the Govan Old Firm game at the end of March.

STEPHEN HUGHES

Stephen Hughes was just seventeen years old when he made his Ibrox debut back in May 2000 as a late substitute in the league clash with Hearts. Last season, the midfielder was in the starting line-up for the first time when Forfar came calling on CIS Cup duty in October before returning home with memories of a 6-0 defeat. Three weeks later, the midfielder claimed his first goal of the campaign – and Rangers' first of the ninety minutes – when, with the game in its latter stages, he headed past keeper Preece to break Aberdeen's stubborn resistance at Ibrox. The following Sunday at Easter Road, his stunning injury time strike secured all three points in the closest of 1-0 victories over Hibernian. After picking up an injury during the home clash with Hearts in late December, Hughes did not start another game until the Scottish Cup tie at Celtic Park in March and then, almost one month later, he netted the only goal of the game against Motherwell at Fir Park to give Alex McLeish his first victory at this venue since becoming manager of Rangers. From then, until the end of the 2003/04 campaign, Hughes started every game except the 2-0 home victory over Partick Thistle when he appeared as a second half substitute for Mikel Arteta.

DRAGAN MLADENOVIC

The Serbian international defensive midfielder arrived in Glasgow during Euro 2004 to agree a four-year deal with Rangers. Indeed, it was during the qualifying stages of this same tournament the previous summer that Mladenovic grabbed the headlines when he scored the only goal of the game during the clash with Wales in Belgrade. Manager Alex McLeish had been keeping a close eye on the Red Star Belgrade player for some time and moved to capture his signature after Jan Wouters filed excellent reports on him at the end of last season. The cultured 28-year-old midfielder naturally brings a wealth of top-class experience to this crucial area of the park. Prior to joining his new team-mates for their pre-season training camp in Austria last July, the player travelled to Japan with Serbia for the Kirin Cup tournament.

ALEX RAE

A Rangers supporter all his days, veteran midfielder Alex Rae arrived at Ibrox from Molineux on a two-year contract for the start of Season 2004/05. Despite his former club Wolves being involved in a Premiership relegation battle for much of the previous campaign, the player had enjoyed a marvellously consistent season in the Midlands before fulfilling an ambition and returning to his boyhood favourites. Rae spent two years, in the 1980s, as an apprentice at the club after earlier star displays with the Celtic Boys' Club team. In early May, prior to joining the club, Rae said, 'I'm coming back up to do my very best. Every time I've joined a big club in England, the fans have taken to me. If I keep doing what I've been doing all these years, then I'm certain the Rangers fans will realise I'm up to the standards of the club.' Appointed Club Vice-Captain for season 2004/05.

GAVIN RAE

Joined Rangers from Dundee at the turn of
the year during the transfer window and,
although not fully fit, made an immediate
debut at Celtic Park in the January league
clash. Unfortunately, the Scotland
international succumbed to a hamstring
injury in the first-half and had to be
substituted. Rae's next start was the Old
Firm Scottish Cup clash in the east end of
Glasgow two months later. Two weeks
after that, the midfielder scored his first
goal for the club when Dundee were sent
back to Dens Park nursing the hangover of
a 4-0 defeat. His second Ibrox goal was a
searing penalty box drive past his close

friend Jamie Langfield in the Partick Thistle goal as Rangers triumphed 2-0
on a particularly wet and miserable April day in Glasgow. The following
week at Tannadice, in the league game with Dundee United, his season
ended prematurely when he was carried off early in the second half with
knee ligament damage. This serious injury would keep him sidelined for
several months.

ROSS McCORMACK

Another member of the highly rated group
of Ibrox youngsters is 17-year-old striker
Ross McCormack who has been hitting the
back of the net on a regular basis for both
the under-19 and under-21 sides.
Something of a dead ball specialist,
McCormack certainly impressed when he
appeared as a second half substitute in the
4-0 triumph over Motherwell at Ibrox in
early May. On the very last day of the
league season, McCormack was in the
starting line-up at East End Park and
scored the winner from the penalty spot
(after he had been brought down by former
Ranger Barry Nicholson) in the 3-2 victory
over Dunfermline.

THE MANAGERS QUIZ

1. Who was manager when Rangers won the first-ever Premier League set-up of ten teams playing each other four times in a season?

2. Name all the managers who have achieved domestic trebles.

3. What was unique about Bill Struth's side in Season 1929/30?

4. Graeme Souness joined Rangers after playing with which Serie A outfit in Italy?

5. When his side won the championship in May 1987, it was the first time that Rangers had won the league in how many years?

6. Name the only man who has been a Rangers manager twice.

7. What was unusual about Willie Thornton's brief spell as interim manager after the departure of Davie White in November 1969?

8. Before arriving at Ibrox, Walter Smith was assistant manager at which club?

9. The legendary Bill Struth was an Edinburgh man and a stonemason by trade. True or false?

10. Who was in charge of Rangers from 1978 to 1983?

ANSWERS ON PAGE 60

RANGERS AND THE DOMESTIC CUPS QUIZ
SEASON 2003/04

1. Rangers were drawn at home to which Second Division club when they entered the CIS Cup competition at the third round stage?

2. Who scored a rare hat-trick that night?

3. Which team provided the opposition in the next round of this competition?

4. His second goal for Rangers was netted in the above tie. His first-ever goal for the club came in the previous round of the same competition. Name him.

5. Stefan Klos kept goal for Rangers in both the third and fourth round ties of the CIS Insurance Cup. True or false?

6. Name the player who netted his first goal in two months in the CIS Cup semi-final against Hibernian.

7. How many penalties did Rangers miss in the above Hampden clash?

8. Which SPL side played host to Rangers in the third round of the Scottish Cup?

9. Who scored for the Light Blues that Saturday?

10. Rangers travelled to Kilmarnock in the next round. Who claimed the opening goal in the 2-0 victory?

ANSWERS ON PAGE 60

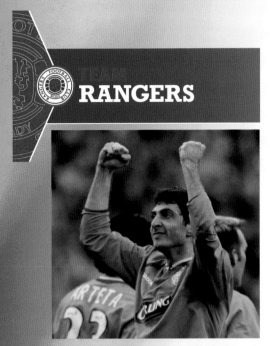

SHOTA ARVELADZE

The Georgian international started last season on fire and scored in three of his first four outings at the beginning of the 2003/04 campaign. His first goal last term was, of course, that rather special volley near the end of the European game with FC Copenhagen in Denmark that took Rangers through to the group stages of the Champions League tournament. Then he netted in consecutive SPL encounters when both Dundee United (3-1, 31.8.03) and Dunfermline (4-0, 13.9.03) were outplayed before claiming doubles in the championship clashes with Hearts (4-0) and Dundee (3-1) in September. After scoring the equaliser in the 1-1 draw with Motherwell at Fir Park the following month, it was another brace for the striker (a tireless worker for the team all over the park) when Kilmarnock were beaten 3-2 at Rugby Park in November. Although not always filling a striker's role in the Rangers line-up, Arveladze continued to find the net in both the league race (2-1 v Hearts in December, 1-0 v Motherwell - January and 3-0 v Hibernian - February) and the Scottish Cup campaign (2-0 v Hibernian - January and 2-0 v Kilmarnock - February) before injury prematurely ended his season. Indeed, Shota had to take a painkilling injection prior to the Scottish Cup tie at Celtic Park and was obviously not his usual mobile self. A few days later, he headed for Holland and an operation to repair wear and tear in his knee thus ensuring that all will be well for the start of the 2004/05 campaign.

CHRIS BURKE

Now under contract until year 2007, the little Glaswegian winger made an early impact last season when, after appearing as a second half substitute for one Nuno Capucho in the late August SPL clash with Hibernian, he netted Rangers' fifth goal of an excellent afternoon's work. Some weeks later and only days after turning 20, he was in the starting line-up for the December CIS Cup tie with St. Johnstone and virtually set Ibrox alight with a virtuoso performance on the wing. In addition to scoring a superb goal (a quite sublime chip from the edge of the area that was one of the goal-of-the-season candidates), Burke was confirmed as man-of-the-match and given a standing ovation by the home support when he left the field five minutes before the end of the game. Later that same month, in his fifth successive outing, the wee man claimed the winner when Hearts were beaten 2-1 in Govan. Unfortunately, injury struck just three weeks later when he landed badly on his ankle during the first half of the Scottish Cup tie at Easter Road and Chris was sidelined for two months. When he made his first Ibrox appearance after the injury (the 4-0 win over Dundee in late March), he was given a tremendous ovation by the Ibrox regulars who simply relish his no-nonsense direct style of play. At Tannadice in late April, flame-haired Burke was again quite superb and tormented Dundee United full-back Archibald for much of the ninety minutes. One week later, he was the most dangerous player on view and it was another man-of-the-match performance when Motherwell nursed a 4-0 hangover on a glorious sunny day at Ibrox. It was during this SPL clash that the winger delighted the home crowd with an audacious piece of skilful play – taking a difficult cross-field pass on his chest, he coolly flicked the ball over defender Hammell and caught it on the other side, with his marker lost for more than just words! When Rangers travelled to Dunfermline on the last day of the league season, he scored a quite sensational goal with a beautifully judged left-foot chip that completely bamboozled Pars keeper Stillie. Hardly surprisingly, Chris Burke was named Rangers Young Player of the Year for Season 2003/04.

HAMED NAMOUCHI

Born in France of Tunisian parents, the elegant midfielder/attacker (a French under-18 international) arrived at the club from Cannes on a two year deal in the summer of 2003 despite being offered a lucrative contract with Premiership giants Chelsea. After scoring against Celtic in an under-21 Old Firm clash, he subsequently made his Rangers first-team debut at Easter Road in the Scottish Cup game against

Hibernian. Coming off the bench to replace the injured Chris Burke, Namouchi created his side's first goal that day (duly converted by Shota Arveladze) and became the first Moslem of the modern era to wear Rangers' colours. After making a substitute appearance for Nuno Capucho the following month, the youngster scored his first-ever first-team goal when Kilmarnock lost 2-0 at Ibrox in a mid-week SPL clash. He was also amongst the scorers three weeks later, giving his side a 3-1 advantage over Dundee United prior to the interval at Tannadice. Again, it had been a substitute appearance. For the SPL clash with Motherwell the following Saturday, Namouchi was on from the start and netted again when he ran on to a superb Frank de Boer through-ball and blasted past veteran keeper Marshall for Rangers' third goal in the 4-0 victory. Sadly, he sustained ligament damage during the latter stages of this game and missed the final three matches of last season.

From the Trophy Room

BAYERN MUNICH LION 1989

EUROPACUP D. MEISTER
FC BAYERN –
GLASGOW RANGERS
27. 9. 1989

Bayern Munich, without doubt the most famous of all Bundesliga sides,
figure prominently in the Ibrox club's European history. Back in May 1967,
after having disposed of holders Borussia Dortmund in a previous round,
Rangers travelled to Nuremberg to meet the Germans in the final of the Cup
Winners' Cup, only days after Celtic had triumphed in Lisbon. There was
nothing between the teams in the ninety minutes, with a disallowed Roger

Hynd 'goal' one of the main talking points. In extra-time, however, Roth netted the only goal of the game to ensure that the silver was heading in the direction of Munich.

Five years later, in the 1972 semi-final of the same competition, Bayern were beaten 2-0 in front of 80,000 supporters at Ibrox (courtesy of first half goals from defender Sandy Jardine and striker Derek Parlane) following a 1-1 first-leg draw in Germany. One month later, of course, Rangers defeated Moscow Dynamo 3-2 in the Nou Camp Stadium, Barcelona and lifted their first European trophy to date after three final appearances in the Cup Winners' Cup.

After winning the Scottish League Championship for Season 1988/89 (number one of nine-in-a-row), the Rangers side of manager Graeme Souness faced Bayern Munich once again – this time in the first-round of the European Cup. In truth, on this occasion, the Germans were much too strong and won 3-1 quite comfortably in Glasgow. Although Rangers (with main man McCoist still injured) put up a far better showing in the second-leg away tie in Munich's Olympic stadium, a 0-0 score was obviously enough for the Germans to progress to the second round of Europe's most prestigious football competition.

This striking piece of porcelain was presented to Rangers and is constantly admired by visitors to the Trophy Room.

First Leg 13.9.89   **Rangers 1**   **Bayern Munich 3**
(Walters)

RANGERS: Woods, Stevens, Munro, Nisbet, Wilkins, Butcher, Steven, I. Ferguson, D. Ferguson, Johnston and Walters.

Second Leg 27.9.89   **Bayern Munich 0**   **Rangers 0**

RANGERS: Ginzburg, Stevens, Munro, Gough,
Wilkins, Butcher, Steven, I. Ferguson,
Cowan (Drinkell), Johnston and Walters.

PETER LOVENKRANDS

Season 2003/04 began well for the Dane and he duly scored in the opening two encounters with Kilmarnock (4-0, 9.8.03) and FC Copenhagen (1-1, 13.8.03) in Scottish and European campaigns respectively. However, the following month, all talk was of his superb winning strike against Stuttgart (after appearing as a second half substitute) in the Champions League clash when Rangers fought back from the brink of defeat for a famous 2-1 victory. It should not be forgotten that Stuttgart had ended the previous season as runners up in the mighty Bundesliga. Understandably, Ibrox was certainly a great place to be that night and memories were rekindled some months later when Lovenkrands' strike was voted Goal of the Season by the club's supporters. Back on SPL duty, the winger claimed his first double of the period when Hearts were beaten 4-0 at Tynecastle in late September before netting another brace in the 3-0 November Govan victory over Aberdeen. On both occasions, one of his two goals was a header. Following that league triumph over the Dons, Lovenkrands was an ever-present in the team until the game with Partick Thistle at Firhill when, after scoring the only goal of the game, he was stretchered off after being caught late by the home side's Ian Ross. This ankle injury kept him out for several matches and although he returned for the crucial Old Firm Scottish Cup tie at Celtic Park, he was not fully match fit. Two weeks later, the Dane was one of the Ibrox scorers when Jim Duffy's Dundee side were comprehensively beaten 4-0 and then, just three days on, it was a case of two-in-a-row with another goal in the 4-1 defeat of Dunfermline at the same venue. Towards the latter part of last season, Lovenkrands was told to rest completely after seeking specialist advice because of persistent knee pain. He did, however, return for the penultimate game of the season, making a second half substitute appearance in the home clash against Hearts.

STEVEN THOMPSON

Back in September 2003 - after giving Rangers an early lead in the game with Dunfermline at Ibrox - fans' favourite Steven Thompson had to leave the field midway though the first period with the recurrence of a pre-season knee injury. Little did the striker realise at the time that it would be several months before he played again. Fast forward to late February 2004 and the SPL Glasgow clash with Hibernian when, after making a second half substitute appearance, the big man duly converted (to great acclaim) a late penalty in the 3-0 win. Thompson was back! He then made the starting line-up for the home game with Dundee (4-0, 20.3.04) and celebrated the occasion with his side's fourth goal of a good afternoon's work. One week later, he came off the bench to score Rangers' first and ultimately only Old Firm goal of the season (a powerful penalty box header from Chris Burke's penetrating corner kick) in the 2-1 Ibrox defeat. Then, in the last game before the league split, the striker opened the scoring against Partick Thistle at Ibrox (Rangers eventually won 2-0) before going one better at Tannadice the following week when his brace put the visitors 2-1 ahead in a fiery encounter that finally ended 3-3. Continuing this fine vein of scoring form the next Saturday, Thompson's tally rose to four in three games with a delightful glancing header (from Paulo Vanoli's cross) in the 4-0 home win over Motherwell. The striker then missed the last game of the season after sustaining an ankle injury against visitors Hearts in the penultimate league clash of the 2003/04 campaign.

RANGERS

NACHO NOVO

In early July 2004, some days after transfer discussions with Old Firm rivals Celtic, 25-year-old Spanish striker Nacho Novo put pen to paper and agreed a four-year deal with Rangers - to the understandable delight of all follow-followers. Brave, confident and extremely fast, the wee man (expected to partner Dado Prso in attack) netted a most impressive 25 goals for his previous club Dundee in the 2003/04 campaign. Indeed, one of these was at Ibrox in late September when the SPL visitors from Dens Park lost 3-1 in an early season league clash. After signing the player, manager Alex McLeish said, 'Nacho has great pace and you know that pace will frighten defenders. He has scored a lot of goals since coming to Scotland and we feel he can definitely help Rangers. We are confident that with the right supply and Nacho's great pace and sharpness in the box that he can score goals.' At the same time, Novo himself commented, 'I always need to prove that I'm good enough to play. I made a good decision when I came to Scotland and now Rangers is an ideal club to join.'

DADO PRSO

With several top clubs including AC Milan, Bolton and Galatasaray after his services, there is no doubt that the capture of Croatian international striker Dado Prso was something of a coup for Rangers. At the time his signing was announced in early May, the 29-year-old had scored seven 2003/04 Champions' League goals for finalists Monaco (including four in the astonishing 8-3 destruction of Deportivo La Coruna) in addition to eight league goals from only sixteen starts for that season's French championship contenders. Prior to the 2004 Champions' League Final against Porto, only his team-mate Fernando Morientes had scored more in that season's competition. As John Collins, former Monaco star, said at the time, 'If Rangers create chances, Prso will take them.' After spells as a youngster with both Hajduk Split and NK Pazinka in Croatia, his family left the country during the troubles between the former Yugoslav republics and moved to France. Later, in 1996, he joined Monaco where he remained for eight years before accepting Rangers' offer of a three-year-deal commencing Season 2004/05. Last March, Prso (nicknamed 'the Croatian Van Basten') won his first cap for his country (against Belgium) and indeed scored on his international debut in the 4-0 win. The striker's call-up to the Croatian squad was partly based on the fact that he had netted twelve times in twenty league games for Monaco. Subsequently, he achieved heroic status in his homeland after netting crucial strikes in both legs of the Euro 2004 play-off with Slovenia (1-1 and 1-0), ensuring that Croatia would line up in Portugal with the rest of Europe's football elite for last summer's tournament.

From the Trophy Room

Following Rangers' famous Scottish Championship win of Season 1974/75 (famous because it finally ended Celtic's long run of successive triumphs), the Ibrox side therefore qualified for the 1975/76 European Cup. After disposing of Bohemians of Dublin 5-2 on aggregate in the first round, Rangers' were then paired with the French champions St. Etienne who presented this genuine miner's lamp to the club as a reminder of the occasion.

Just prior to kick-off in the first-leg in France, Rangers were dealt an early blow when first choice keeper Peter McCloy was injured during the warm-up. Stewart Kennedy took his place in the starting line-up. Despite 'Les Verts' (the Greens) dominating the first period and taking the lead through Patrick Revelli in some twenty-five minutes, the visitors began to look the part as they pushed hard for an equaliser. As the second half progressed, a Rangers goal looked more and more a possibility but it was not to be and, to make matters much worse, poor defending in the last minute of regulation time saw the home side double their tally to two.

Two weeks later in Glasgow, it was an altogether different story - Rangers were simply outclassed. St. Etienne again scored twice before Alex MacDonald netted a consolation goal right at the end of the game. That season, the French side went all the way to the final of the competition, returning to Glasgow in due course for this Hampden event. On that occasion, however, their Scottish trip was not so fruitful and old friends Bayern Munich defeated them 1-0 to take the trophy to Germany.

Although there was disappointment on the European stage, Rangers completed a clean sweep domestically that season with a treble of League Championship, Scottish Cup and League Cup.

First Leg 22.10.75   St. Etienne 2   Rangers 0

RANGERS: Kennedy, Jardine, Miller, Greig, Jackson, Forsyth, McLean, Stein, Parlane, MacDonald and Johnstone.

Second Leg 5.11.75   Rangers 1   St. Etienne 2
(MacDonald)

RANGERS: Kennedy, Jardine, Greig, Forsyth, Jackson, MacDonald, McLean, Stein, Parlane, Johnstone and Young.

STRIKING GOLD

MARK HATELEY

When Mark Hateley first wore the blue of Rangers, at the start of the 1990/91 campaign, he was regularly singled out for criticism by a section of the follow-follow brigade. In truth, the striker was far from 100% fit, having spent much of the previous year at Monaco trying to shake off a troublesome ankle injury. However, those jeers soon turned to cheers and, by the end of his first season, Hateley was well on his way to the Ibrox Hall of Fame when his two goals against Aberdeen (in the very last league game of the season) delivered championship number three of the 'nine-in-a-row' sequence.

The big man's next campaign began with a hat-trick in the St. Johnstone game and then, on a hot August afternoon, the striker claimed both goals at Celtic Park in the 2-0 Old Firm victory. By the following May, Rangers added the Scottish Cup (for the first time since 1981) to the League Championship with the Englishman scoring the Hampden opener as Airdrie were beaten 2-1.

In Season 1992/93, the player provided a seemingly endless list of football highlights. Few will ever forget: the magnificent twenty-five yard left-foot volley against Leeds at Elland Road in the European Cup, the inch-perfect curling cross for Ally's diving header and goal number two in the same game, Mark's own headed equaliser against Marseille that almost took the roof of Ibrox and the superb run and sweet low drive from an acute angle for Rangers second and decisive goal in the Scottish Cup Final triumph over Aberdeen. Sweet, sweet memories!

By now, he was the most feared striker in Scottish Football and, at the end of Season 1993/94, was voted Player of the Year by Scottish Football Writers' Association thus becoming the first Englishman to win this prestigious award. Hateley had totalled

30 goals in all competitions that year, with closest rivals Aberdeen and Celtic suffering again. For example, in the Ne'er Day derby at Celtic Park, his opener in the first minute of play set Rangers up for a convincing 4-2 win.

Sadly, injury was to play a part in his last year with the club and, at the beginning of the 1995/96 period, he joined Queen's Park Rangers, then bossed by former colleague Ray Wilkins. That was not quite the end of the story, however, as Mark did return briefly to help the cause just prior to the 'nine-in-a-row' decider at Celtic Park in March 1997.

When asked at the time how it felt to be coming back, the big man simply replied 'Coming back? No, I'm coming home.' And that really said it all.

THE MAGNIFICENT 7

When Rangers lifted all three domestic trophies of League Championship, Scottish Cup and League (CIS) Cup in Season 1992/93, it was the seventh time in the club's proud history that this special 'triple crown' feat had been recorded. Here's a reminder of each of those seven magnificent seasons:

SEASON 1948/49

Following the introduction of the League Cup competition for Season 1946/47 (the Light Blues beat Aberdeen in the final), the Rangers team of legendary manager Bill Struth (who once famously said 'Let the others come after us. We welcome the chase.') became the first-ever Scottish side to secure the treble, two seasons later. Although the section stage of the League Cup started badly with draws against Clyde (home) and Hibernian (away) as well as a 3-1 Old Firm defeat in the east end of Glasgow, results improved and Celtic were beaten 2-1 (in

BILL STRUTH
MANAGER OF RANGERS
18 League Championships, 10 Scottish Cups, 2 League Cups, 18 Glasgow Cups, 20 Glasgow Charity Cups

front of an astonishing 105,000 fans!) in what was really the section decider at Ibrox. Later, on final day in March, Rangers defeated Raith Rovers 2-0. In the league, it was very much a two horse race with closest rivals Dundee only needing a point in the last game at Falkirk to claim the title. They lost and, with Rangers winning 4-1 at Stirling Albion, the championship returned to the Trophy Room.

The Scottish Cup Final was played the week before the above league encounter, with Rangers beating Clyde 4-1 at Hampden to retain the trophy. One of the scorers that day was Billy Williamson who was making his first Scottish Cup appearance of the season. In the same competition the previous year, he had netted the winner for Rangers in the 1-0 final with Morton. Amazingly, that too had been his first Scottish Cup appearance of the season!

SEASON 1963/64

RALPH BRAND scores against Celtic

Unbeaten in the section stage of the League Cup (Celtic suffered 3-0 defeats both home and away), second division Morton were crushed 5-0 in the final of the competition. Cousins Jim Forrest and Alec Willoughby shared the goals between them with Forrest netting four (a cup final record by a Rangers man) and his relative the other.

Kilmarnock pushed Rangers hard in the league and, indeed, actually led the race at one point during the campaign. However, the Ayrshire club's challenge was virtually ended by a 2-0 Glasgow defeat in mid March as Scot Symon's side headed for their third championship in just four seasons, not knowing that it would be eleven long years before the championship flag was unfurled again.

With Partick Thistle (3-0), Celtic (2-0) and Dunfermline (1-0) all failing to halt the team's Scottish Cup progress on the road to Hampden, nearly 121,000 spectators gathered at the National Stadium for the Rangers/Dundee clash in late April. In one of the truly great Scottish Cup Finals, the Ibrox men left it late to snatch victory but, with two goals in the last two minutes, the destination of the trophy was finally settled following a 3-1 victory. Ralph Brand, one of the scorers that day, became the first player to score in three successive Scottish Cup Finals.

SEASON 1975/76

After disposing of lowly Queen of the South and Montrose in the quarter-final and semi-final of the League Cup respectively, far tougher opposition, in the shape of Celtic, provided the Hampden opposition at the ultimate stage of this competition in October 1975. The game (and the trophy) was won by midfielder Alex MacDonald's flying, second half header which ignited the blue touchpaper at one end of the National Stadium.
In the championship, Jock Wallace's Rangers went on an unbeaten run from early December until the end of the campaign with the Celtic clash at Ibrox, near the start of this sequence, proving to be crucial. Prior to this game, their Old Firm rivals were three points ahead but a 1-0 victory (courtesy of striker Derek Johnstone's goal) narrowed the gap at the top of the table. The league title was eventually secured against Dundee United at Tannadice when Johnstone was again the only scorer of the game but this time in the first minute of play. Closest challengers Celtic ended the season six points behind in second place.
One week after the aforementioned Tayside encounter, the treble was in the bag when Hearts were beaten 3-1 in the Scottish Cup Final. Amazingly, Derek Johnstone again netted in the first minute of play to record a rather unique double – in successive weeks and in the very first minute of trophy-deciding games, his name was on crucial goals.

SEASON 1977/78

This season's League Cup Final was also against Celtic although the game went into extra-time before Rangers eventually triumphed 2-1. Goals from Gordon Smith and the legendary Davie Cooper did the damage. Following an earlier 6-1 defeat of Aberdeen in the same competition, manager Billy McNeill had suggested that this was the best display of football he had ever witnessed by an Ibrox side.
Indeed, it was the team from the north who proved to be closest rivals in the league race, having defeated Rangers in three of the four championship encounters. However, one point ahead with three games left, Rangers won all their remaining fixtures for championship number 37. At the end of the day, Celtic were nowhere to be seen and languished in fifth place when hostilities finally ended. Earlier, in the first Old Firm game of the season, they had actually led 2-0 at half-time but a superb second period of three goals by Rangers turned the match on its head.
Maybe not surprisingly, it was Aberdeen who took to the field with Rangers on Scottish Cup Final day but the close 2-1 score fails to convey the fact

that the Pittodrie side were simply outplayed at Hampden. With two trebles in just three years, Jock Wallace's side had become immortal.

SEASON 1992/93

Fifteen years on, it was Aberdeen that offered the toughest domestic opposition once again for the majority of this 1992/93 campaign and, for the fourth time in just six years, they clashed with Rangers in the final of the League Cup competition. In an extremely close-fought encounter, Stuart McColl's opener had been cancelled out by Duncan Shearer before, in extra-time, a David Robertson cross was deflected past Snelders into the net by Pittoodrie defender

MARK HATELEY celebrates another goal against Celtic

Gary Smith. Showing remarkable consistency, Walter Smith's Rangers went on a tremendous run in the league and, after losing 4-3 away to Dundee in mid-August, were beaten only once before securing the championship at Broomfield in May when Gary McSwegan's goal earned maximum points in the clash with Airdrie. With Ally McCoist and Mark Hateley top scorers on 34 and 21 respectively, the team ended the campaign nine points in front of second place Aberdeen.

Indeed it was the Pittodrie outfit who joined the champions at Celtic Park (Hampden was being renovated) to contest the Scottish Cup Final. Although the final 2-1 score was the same as the earlier League Cup clash, on this occasion the game was dominated by Rangers with both Neil Murray and Hateley (a wonderful strike on the run) netting as the fans celebrated the bluest of days.

SEASON 1998/99

Number six of the seven was just a wee bit more special with the first part of the treble being hailed when St. Johnstone (also Scottish Cup semi-final opponents later that same season) were defeated 2-1 in the final of the League Cup at Celtic Park. The scorers that day were French striker Guivar'ch and a certain German midfielder

Neil McCann

whose name still evokes such wonderful memories for all follow-followers – Jorg Albertz.

Since the formation of the Scottish League over 100 years previously, no Rangers side had ever won the League Championship at the home of their greatest rivals but, on 2 May, 1999, that is exactly what Dick Advocaat's side achieved at Celtic Park in the last Old Firm encounter of the campaign. The game, a fiery and controversial clash, was won 3-0 with Neil McCann (a double) and Albertz (again) the goal heroes. Captain Lorenzo Amoruso also entered the record books and became the first foreign player to skipper Rangers to Scotland's top domestic honour.

The Scottish Cup Final at the 'new' Hampden also involved Celtic but, on this occasion, the game was a more subdued affair with striker Rod Wallace (who had been dismissed near the end of championship winning encounter in the east end of Glasgow) claiming the only goal of the ninety minutes.

SEASON 2002/03

Alex McLeish joined the ranks of the great Ibrox managers when he led Rangers to the domestic treble in period 2002/03. The League Cup was won for the twenty-third time after old friends Celtic fell 2-1 at the National Stadium following first half goals from Claudio Caniggia and Peter Lovenkrands. The Dane had now scored the winner in the last two Hampden cup finals with Celtic.

In the closest league race for many, many years, the destination of the flag was still in

BARRY FERGUSON with SPL Trophy

doubt right up until the final whistle of the last game of the season and came down to goal difference between the Old Firm giants. With Rangers beating Dunfermline 6-1 at Ibrox, their tally of 101 goals scored and 28 goals conceded (as opposed to Celtic's 98 and 26 respectively) was just enough for the rejoicing to begin.

Maybe it was fitting that Lorenzo Amoruso, who had been immense all season, should claim the Hampden winner against Dundee six days later in the Scottish Cup Final as the Italian defender was playing his last game for the club before moving to Blackburn Rovers in the English Premiership. It was a perfect end to another perfect day in another perfect season!

THE MAGNIFICENT 7

HEADLINE NEWS

RANGERS MADE THE FOLLOWING FOOTBALL HEADLINES DURING SEASON 2003/04.

WHAT WAS THE OCCASION?   THE CLUE IS IN THE DATE!

1 'NORTHERN FIGHTS' Sunday Herald, 17.8.03

2 'FEAST OF STEPHEN' Sunday Mirror, 23.11.03

3 'A GREEK TRAGEDY' Daily Mail, 2.10.03

4 'CHRISTIAN SLAYS LIONS' Sunday Mirror, 25.1.04

5 'MAKING WAVES IN THE DEEP END' Daily Mail, 17.9.03

6 'A SAFER BET NOW' Daily Mail, 24.3.04

7 'KLOS CALL AS TETCHY RANGERS END JINX'
Daily Mail, 5.4.04

8 'HUGHES SOMEHOW HANGS ON IN THERE' Daily Mail, 1.12.03

9 'GORDON TAKES A GRIP TO BREAK IBROX HEARTS'
Mail on Sunday, 14.3.04

10 'HOME COMFORTS'
Mail on Sunday, 18.4.04

ANSWERS ON PAGE 60

From the Trophy Room

THE MOSES McNEIL TROPHY 1876

Although won by Moses McNeil, one of the club's founders, this almost priceless Trophy Room exhibit is actually from a local athletics meeting.

Back in 1872, sixteen-year-old Moses (along with his brother Peter and friends Peter Campbell and William McBeath) decided to form a football club at a time when, although the sport of football was indeed growing, it was still in its infancy in Scotland. So it came to pass that 'Rangers' were born - with the name coming from an English rugby club that Moses had heard of at the time. With the other members all under twenty, the lads trained hard for several weeks before their first 'official' outing against Callendar FC in May 1872 and a 0-0 draw. The line-up for that first historic game not only included Moses but also Peter, William and Harry, three of his other six brothers.

Capped for Scotland in 1876, Moses was the club's first international player. A strong powerful winger, he was also a member of the first-ever Rangers Scottish Cup Final side when, in front of some 15,000 spectators, favourites Vale of Leven eventually lifted the trophy after a 3-2 second replay victory in 1877. McNeil's name was on one of his side's two goals that April day. Two years later, with Vale of Leven again the opponents on

Cup Final day, officials ordered a replay despite claims by Rangers that the result was 2-1 in their favour as opposed to a 1-1 draw. With the Light Blues then refusing to turn up for the rematch, Vale of Leven were presented with the trophy - as Moses and his team mates spent the day at Ayr Races!

Moses (centre) in team of
1876-77

William Wilton (Match Secretary 1891-1899 and Manager 1899-1920)
10 League Championships and 4 Scottish Cups

William Struth (1920-1954)
18 League Championships, 10 Scottish Cups and 2 League Cups
The Victory Cup (1946)

Scot Symon (1954-1967)
6 League Championships, 5 Scottish Cups and 4 League Cups

Willie Waddell (1969-1972)
European Cup Winners' Cup and 1 League Cup

Jock Wallace (1972-1978 and 1983-1986)
3 League Championships, 3 Scottish Cups and 4 League Cups

& WINNERS

John Greig (1978-1983)
2 Scottish Cups and 2 League Cups

Graeme Souness (1986-1991)
3 League Championships and 4 League Cups

Walter Smith (1991-1998)
7 League Championships, 3 Scottish Cups and 3 League Cups

Dick Advocaat (1998-2001)
2 League Championships, 2 Scottish Cups and 1 League Cup

Alex McLeish (2001-)
1 League Championship, 2 Scottish Cups and 2 League Cups

STRIKING GOLD

JIM FORREST

With striker Jimmy Millar out at the start of the 1963/64 period, youngster Jim Forrest (who had been signed from Glasgow Schools in 1960) was given the opportunity of securing a regular place in Rangers starting line-up. In the first game of that season, he duly scored a double as Celtic were beaten 3-0 in the League Cup and then, as the Ibrox club headed for a final showdown, he grabbed another ten goals on the road to Hampden. A crowd of nearly 106,000 watched the ultimate game in this competition when Forrest earned a place in the

record books with four goals to his name in the 5-0 beating of Morton. Alec Willoughby, his cousin, was the other scorer for Rangers that day.

In many ways, Forrest had it all - he was fast, brave, good in the air, superbly balanced and a deadly finisher with either foot. By the end of 1963/64, a domestic treble had been won for the first time in fifteen years but Forrest missed the last few games of the League and Scottish Cup campaigns after being carried off at Pittodrie in March. Prior to that injury, he had hit 21 goals in 24 championship games as well as scoring in the 2-0 quarter-final Scottish Cup triumph over Celtic.

The following 1964/65 period was even better for the player and Jim created a club record of 57 goals in all games with 40 of those coming before Christmas. Although there were no championship celebrations that year, the striker claimed all his side's goals in both the League Cup 2-1 semi-final defeat of Dundee United and the 2-1 final beating of Celtic as Rangers retained the trophy.

Then, after a total of 35 strikes in the three 1965/66 domestic competitions, his Ibrox career came to an abrupt halt after the Scottish Cup defeat at Berwick in January of the next year. Unfairly, the blame for this embarrassing first round exit at the hands of a team from a lower division landed at the feet of both Forrest and inside-forward George McLean. Neither kicked a ball in earnest for the club again and Forrest left to join Preston North End shortly afterwards in March.

It seemed obvious, even at the time, that Rangers had made a major error in transferring the player in such haste. This rush to judgement may just have cost the club their first European trophy as two months later in Nuremberg (in the final of the European Cup Winners' Cup with Bayern Munich), his natural ability in front of goal was sadly missed.

THE QUOTES QUIZ

1 'OF COURSE, IT WAS WONDERFUL TO GET A CHANCE TO GO TO CHELSEA, WITH EVERYTHING THAT HAS BEEN GOING ON THERE THIS YEAR, BUT I HAD TO DECIDE WHAT WAS BEST FOR ME. I HAVE FOUND THE GAME A GOOD BIT MORE PHYSICAL AND FRANTIC HERE. THE TEMPO AND STYLE ARE ALTOGETHER DIFFERENT IN FRANCE, BUT I'VE BEEN ABLE TO GET USED TO IT.'

'IT'S FANTASTIC — I LIKE THE WAY THE FANS HERE LOVE THE GAME AS A SPORT. IN ITALY, THE FANS ARE MORE LIKE DIRECTORS THESE DAYS, THEY'VE LOST THEIR IDENTITY, WITH ALL THE PROBLEMS IN THE ITALIAN GAME.' **2**

3

'HE'S ULTRA-COOL BUT HE COMMANDS GREAT RESPECT. HE'S GOT A PRESENCE, AN AURA WHEN HE WALKS IN THE ROOM. MAYBE I DIDN'T REALISE HOW GOOD HE WAS WHEN I CAME HERE.'

4

'I HAVE ONLY GOOD MEMORIES OF MY TIME IN GLASGOW. IT HAS BEEN AN HONOUR AND A PRIVILEGE TO PLAY FOR RANGERS BUT IT IS DEFINITELY THE RIGHT DECISION TO LEAVE.'

5 'IT WAS LOVELY TO GET AN OVATION FROM THE FANS AGAINST DUNDEE. IF YOU SAW ME RUNNING ON THE PITCH, I WAS LAUGHING BECAUSE I COULD NOT BELIEVE THE OVATION I GOT. IT'S A BIT MAD ACTUALLY BUT THE FANS HAVE BEEN EXCELLENT TO ME. I JUST HOPE I CAN KEEP ON GIVING THEM WHAT THEY WANT.'

WHO SAID THAT?

6 'HE HAS, OF COURSE, GONE ON TO PROVE HIMSELF IN THE SCOTTISH GAME AND HAS BEEN FORMIDABLE AT THE HEART OF THE LIVINGSTON DEFENCE. HE'S NOW GOT A LOT OF EXPERIENCE UNDER HIS BELT AND WINNING A MEDAL TAKES A PLAYER'S STOCK UP. HE NOW OFFERS SOMETHING WE DON'T HAVE.'

7 'I'M NO FLY-BY-NIGHT, I'M A RANGERS SUPPORTER AND I KNOW WHAT IT'S ALL ABOUT. I'VE BEEN THERE OFTEN ENOUGH. I'VE PICKED UP A COUPLE OF PLAYER OF THE YEAR AWARDS DOWN HERE AND I THINK I'VE DONE THAT WHILE PLAYING IN A BETTER LEAGUE THAN THE SPL. I'VE PUT IN SOME DECENT PERFORMANCES IN A TEAM THAT HAS STRUGGLED ALL SEASON IN THE PREMIERSHIP AND THAT'S THE GAUGE I GO BY, NOT THE DATE ON MY BIRTH CERTIFICATE.'

8 'RANGERS ARE THE CLUB I NEEDED TO JOIN. THEY ARE A CLUB IN MY OWN IMAGE AND THEIR AMBITIONS ARE ON THE SAME LEVEL AS MY OWN. I WAS INSTANTLY WON OVER BY THE WAY THEY BEHAVED TOWARDS ME. THEY PROVIDED ME WITH A PRIVATE JET AND WELCOMED ME IN EXTRAORDINARY FASHION. I STRUCK UP A GREAT RAPPORT WITH ALEX MCLEISH IMMEDIATELY. EVERYTHING WAS SO IMPRESSIVE AND I MADE UP MY MIND TO JOIN THEM STRAIGHT AWAY.'

'MY PARENTS SPLIT UP WHEN I WAS VERY YOUNG AND MY GRAND-MOTHER WAS INSISTENT THAT I GOT A GOOD EDUCATION. SHE BROUGHT ME UP TO PRAY FIRST THING IN THE MORNING AND LAST THING AT NIGHT. SHE GAVE ME MY RELIGIOUS SPIRIT AND TAUGHT ME THE IMPORTANCE OF SEEKING GOD AND BELIEVING IN GOD. FOR THAT GIFT ALONE, I WILL BE ETERNALLY THANKFUL TO HER.'

9

ANSWERS ON PAGE 61

AN A-Z

A is for Advocaat, the club's first foreign manager who, in year one after arriving from Holland, led Rangers to the 1998/99 treble of domestic silverware. When the Championship was won on a glorious afternoon at Celtic Park in early May that season, it was another foreigner - Italian Lorenzo Amoruso – who became not only the first Rangers captain to secure Scotland's top domestic honour at the home of their Old Firm rivals, but also the first foreign player to skipper the club to a league title.

B is for Baxter, the 1960s legend who was just maybe the most naturally gifted Ibrox footballer of them all. Excelling in the heat of the Old firm inferno, he was only on the losing side twice in eighteen clashes (between 1960 and 1965) with the team in green. Most memorably, in the Scottish Cup Final replay of 1963 which Rangers won 3-0, Jim Baxter's complete domination of the midfield helped ensure one of the most one-sided Old Firm encounters for many a long year. He played alongside the deadly penalty box predator Ralph Brand who became the first footballer to score in three successive Scottish Cup Finals when Rangers beat Dundee 3-1 in April 1964. Additionally, Brand netted six times in seven cup finals for Rangers and was never on the losing side. At the start of the Souness revolution in 1986, Terry Butcher, deputy captain of England, arrived in Glasgow to become, in many ways, the focal point of that new era. Nine months later at Pittodrie, it was Butcher's goal in the 1-1 draw with Aberdeen that secured the required point to give Rangers their first title win in nine long years.

Jim Baxter

OF RANGERS

C is for Caldow, an exceptionally fast full-back who captained both Rangers and Scotland in the late 1950s and early 1960s. Winner of five League Championship medals, Eric missed only two Scotland internationals in the period from April 1957 to April 1963 before tragically breaking his leg in the Wembley game with England in that latter year. Davie Cooper, first and foremost a Rangers man, was a winger of supreme ability and one of the club's most favoured and gifted sons. His performance in the Scottish Cup Final replay of 1981 (Dundee United were beaten 4-1) is the stuff of legend. Davie tragically passed away in March 1995, just a few days after his 39th birthday.

D is for both Dawson and Durrant, 'Prince of Goalkeepers' and 'Blue, White Dynamite' midfielder respectively. Ask any 'old Jimmy' at Ibrox the name of the club's greatest keeper and Jerry Dawson will surely be the reply. Blessed with exceptionally fast reflexes, he was the last line of defence in the 1930s/1940s and won five League Championships, two Scottish Cups, two Scottish War Cups, two Summer War Cups and one Southern League Cup during his 16 years with the club. Govan boy Ian Durrant joined the only team he ever wanted to play for as a schoolboy and, following the arrival of Graeme Souness, made the No. 10 jersey virtually his own. In that 'first' championship season of 1986/87, Durrant wore it with pride on no fewer than 39 league outings. The abiding image of the player, arms aloft in 'Victory V' celebration after scoring, is now part of Ibrox folklore.

Ian Durrant

European Cup Winners' Cup team of 1972

E is for European Cup Winners' Cup which the team lifted in May 1972 after Moscow Dynamo were beaten 3-2 at the Nou Camp Stadium in Barcelona. Goals from Colin Stein and Willie Johnston (a double) started the celebrations. This was the third time that Rangers had reached the ultimate stage of this European competition, having been defeated in previous finals by the Italians of Fiorentina (1961) and the Germans of Bayern Munich in 1967.

F is for all the Fergusons who have worn the blue of Rangers over the years. Long before his managerial career and subsequent knighthood, Alex Ferguson was an Ibrox centre-forward who, for example, scored 19 goals in 29 league appearances in Season 1967/68. Midfielder Ian Ferguson is one of only three Rangers players (the others being Richard Gough and Ally McCoist) who has every medal from the 'nine-in-a-row' sequence of championship successes. Although Derek Ferguson enjoyed success at Ibrox during the Souness era, it was his brother Barry who really captured the hearts of those who follow, follow. After his 'tour de force' performance against Celtic in the Scottish Cup Final of May 2002, Barry was Player of the Year the next season as he led the side to a magnificent domestic treble, netting eighteen precious goals along the way.

Ian Ferguson

G is for Greig, the 'Greatest Ever Ranger' and inspiring club captain who played in an astonishing 857 games during his eighteen years as a player at Ibrox. As well as skippering the side to their European Cup Winners' Cup triumph of 1972, John Greig is the only footballer at the club to have 'won' three separate trebles – in 1963/64, 1975/76 and 1977/78. Twice Scotland's Player of the Year, he retired in 1978 and was then manager of the club for five years. Richard Gough was another great club captain and, indeed, the most successful since the days of Davie Meiklejohn some sixty years earlier. Brave as a lion, the Swedish born defender amassed nine (nine-in-a-row) league championship medals, three Scottish Cup medals and six League Cup medals. The season after Gough was appointed captain, manager Walter Smith brought Andy Goram to Rangers from Hibernian. In due course, 'The Goalie' would become an Ibrox legend with, in particular, his performances in the Old Firm clashes with Celtic still talked about by the fans to this day. Walter Smith also brought the wayward genius Paul Gascoigne to

John Greig

Glasgow. At the end of his first season in Govan, a stunning hat-trick against Aberdeen in late April secured championship flag No 46 and, although controversy seemed to follow him everywhere, few will ever forget his major contribution to two championships in three seasons.

H is for Henderson who, back in the 1960s, was one of the true, genuine characters of the Scottish game. Standing at only five foot four inches, winger 'Wee Willie' Henderson was fast, strong and an expert dribbler whose superb crosses were like food and drink to strikers Millar and Brand.

I is naturally for Ibrox Stadium. With its imposing red brick façade, the Main Stand (then known as the Grandstand) was officially opened on New Year's Day 1929 when visitors Celtic were beaten 3-0. Following the disaster in 1971 when 66 Rangers fans lost their lives, three new stands were then built and opened in August 1979 (Copeland Road Stand), August 1980 (Broomloan Road Stand) and December 1981 (Govan Stand) with the completion of the Club Deck, on top of the Main Stand, in 1991. Incidentally, the Main Stand was given listed building status in 1980.

J is for Johnstone, with or without an e. At just sixteen years old, Derek Johnstone became the youngest player to score the winning goal in a cup final when his header at Hampden against Celtic brought the League Cup (Rangers' first silverware in four years) back to the Trophy Room in October 1970. DJ also won Scottish Cup medals in three different positions – centre-forward, centre-half and midfield! In the European Cup Winners' Cup campaign of 1971/72, winger Willie Johnston not only claimed a double in the final but also scored priceless earlier round away goals in the clashes with Rennes (1-1) and Torino (1-1). Danish defender Kai

Johansen famously scored the winner in a rather important Old Firm encounter when his thunderous twenty-five yard drive won the Scottish Cup in April 1966. Just like Derek Johnstone and Willie Johnston, full-back Sandy Jardine was a member of the side that triumphed in Europe in 1972 – indeed he had scored the opener in the 2-0 semi-final win over favourites Bayern Munich at Ibrox. The cultured defender simply oozed class and played over 670 official games for Rangers, collecting three championship and five Scottish Cup medals along the way.

Derek Johnstone

K is for Kitchenbrand - a South African striker who scored 24 goals in 25 games in Season 1955/56. Nicknamed 'The Rhino' for the most obvious of reasons, Don Kitchenbrand hit five goals past Queen of the South during the very first Scottish League match to be played by floodlight.

L can only be for Laudrup, a true genius who graced the Ibrox turf for three glorious years. It was his flashing header at Tannadice in May 1997 that finally made 'nine-in-a-row' become reality but, one year earlier on a warm Hampden afternoon, the Danish superstar had been even more impressive when he dismantled Hearts in the final of the Scottish Cup. Brian not only scored twice that day but also created the other three in the 5-1 triumph, his greatest hour in Scottish Football.

Brian Laudrup

M is for the magical McCoist who won Europe's 'Golden Boot' award for both the 1991/92 and 1992/93 periods, becoming the only player to retain this prestigious trophy. In the 1991/92 campaign, Ally not only reached a career total of 200 league goals but also claimed Rangers 100th for the season whilst in Season 1992/93, he hit 34 goals in 34 league games before breaking his leg in Portugal on duty with Scotland. Who will ever forget the diving header that silenced the Leeds fans at Elland Road in the 1992 European Cup tie or the audacious overhead kick that won the League Cup for

Ally McCoist

Rangers in the 1993 final with Hibernian? Just two wonderful memories from a book full of them. Fiery midfielder Alex MacDonald scored the winner against Celtic in the final of the League Cup in October 1975, the first stage of treble success that season. Very few players could distribute a football with the uncanny accuracy of winger Tommy McLean who was a member of the same team. Dubbed 'The Wee Prime Minister' because of the way he controlled the team back in the early 1960s, the superbly gifted Ian McMillan played alongside Jim Baxter in what many consider to be one of Rangers finest-ever teams. A chartered surveyor, he remained a part-time player throughout his Ibrox career. There's also, of course, current manager Alex McLeish who led his players to a domestic cup double in his first season at the club and then, the following year, that memorable treble (the club's seventh in total) for period 2002/03. Quite rightly, now a legend, Govan born Davie Meiklejohn was at the club from 1919 to 1936 (playing 635 games) and scored the crucial opening goal (a penalty) at Hampden against Celtic in the 1928 Scottish Cup Final when Rangers ended their 25 year hoodoo in this competition. Although not the regular penalty-kicker, defender 'Meek' felt that, as captain, the responsibility was his. The rest, as they say, is history. Also in the team that day was the finest footballer of his generation, winger Alan Morton who was famously nicknamed 'Wee Blue Devil' after his part in the demolition of England at Wembley in 1928 when Scotland won 5-1. To this day, Morton's oil portrait takes pride of place above the splendid marble staircase inside the main entrance at Ibrox Stadium. In the Scottish Cup run of 1960, centre-forward Jimmy Millar headed the equaliser (from all of sixteen yards) in the semi-final with Celtic. After claiming two more in the 4-1 replay victory, his name was on both goals when Kilmarnock lost 2-0 in the final!

N is for George Niven – an exceptionally brave goalkeeper who was carried off with a head injury in the first half of the 1953 Scottish Cup Final against Aberdeen. Returning for the second period swathed in bandages (after stitches both outside and inside his ear), he was outstanding. At one time or another during his Rangers career (five championships, two Scottish Cups and one League Cup), ex-miner Niven fractured arms, wrists, fingers, shoulders and jaw!

O is for the Osasuna Bull, a Spanish gift of porcelain and one of the many fascinating items on display in the Ibrox Trophy Room. Opened in 1959 to house the club's growing treasure trove of memorabilia and silverware, the Trophy Room remains the crowning glory of the stadium.

Derek Parlane

P is for both Parlane and Provan, striker and full-back respectively. Derek Parlane was just eighteen years old when he scored against Bayern Munich at Ibrox in the semi-final of the 1971/72 European Cup Winners' Cup. He also claimed the club's 6000th league goal on the day that he scored all four in the 4-2 victory over Hearts in January 1974. Defender Davie Provan (with the club from 1958 to 1970) was a superbly balanced player equally at home on either the right or left side of defence. Prior to first-team activity, Provan had spent five patient years in the reserves awaiting his chance.

Q In May 1973, the Queen's cousin, Princess Alexandra, became the first-ever member of the royal family to attend the Scottish Cup Final. Rangers won a quite marvellous Old Firm encounter 3-2 with defender Tom Forsyth netting the winner (his first goal for the club) in front of nearly 123,000 spectators. Indeed, it was the last final to be played in front of a six-figure crowd.

R is for the duo of Russell and Roberts. An absolute joy to watch, right midfielder Bobby Russell exuded class and scored the winner in Holland on the night that PSV Eindhoven were beaten at home for the very first time in European competition back in Season 1978/79. This 3-2 triumph was one of Rangers' greatest ever victories on foreign soil. Choir master, conductor and guest goalkeeper Graham Roberts will always be remembered by the Ibrox legions as a player who never gave less than 100%. Whatever else, the Rangers cause was all that mattered to him and, despite barely two seasons in Glasgow from 1986 to 1988, the Englishman is still revered down Govan way.

S is for four managers with the names of Struth, Symon, Souness and Smith. Their records are as follows: Bill Struth (1920-1954) – 18 League Championships, 10 Scottish Cups and 2 League Cups. Scot Symon (1954-1967) – 6 League Championships, 5 Scottish Cups and 4 League Cups. Graeme Souness (1986-1992) – 3 League Championships and 4 League Cups. Walter Smith (1991-1998) – 7 League Championships, 3 Scottish Cups and 3 League Cups.

T is for Tiger – the Ibrox variety! Winner of four League Titles, three Scottish Cups and two League Cups, club captain Jock 'Tiger' Shaw was an unbelievable forty-two years old when he retired as a Rangers player in 1954 after the club's North American Tour. Indeed, when he led his side to successive league and cup doubles in 1948/49 and 1949/50, he was a mere youngster in his late thirties.....and still a tiger in the tackle!

U is for the UEFA Cup, a tournament Rangers first entered in Season 1982/83. Following an aggregate 3-0 victory over Borussia Dortmund in the first round, another German side in the shape of FC Cologne proved too strong and crushed Rangers 5-0 on their own patch after losing 2-1 in Govan two weeks earlier.

V is for Valletta and Vladikavkaz, foreign sides that have both conceded ten goals to Rangers in Europe. In the European Cup of 1990/91, Valletta of Malta lost 6-0 and 4-0 over two legs and then, in the preliminary round of the same competition in Season 1996/97, the Russian champions of Vladikavkaz were defeated not only 3-1 at Ibrox but also 7-2 in front of their own fans.

W is for Waddell who was not only an integral part of the great post-war Rangers side that dominated Scottish Football in the late forties and early fifties (he won four championships and two Scottish Cups during that time) but also team manager when the Light Blues triumphed on the European stage in 1972. Few have served the club as well as Willie Waddell. Another legendary manager was Jock Wallace, a hard man who guided the

Willie Waddell   Jock Wallace

club in both 1972 to 1978 and 1983 to 1986 and won two domestic trebles during his first period in charge. Many Rangers fans, of course, knew of him prior to his Ibrox arrival as Jock had been Berwick goalkeeper on 28th January 1967, the day that his side dramatically knocked Rangers out of the Scottish Cup at the first round stage. A member of the remarkable post-war 'Iron Curtain' defence, centre-half Willie Woodburn was a truly magnificent player whose game was virtually faultless. He also had a quite simple philosophy – little else was of concern but Rangers success.

X is for eX Celt Maurice Johnston whose arrival at Ibrox in 1989 certainly made all the headlines. The striker made nearly as many again when he scored the winner against his old side (and was booked for his celebrations) just three months later in the 1-0 league victory. Johnston went on to win two league titles whilst wearing light blue and, in truth, played for the jersey as if to the manor born.

Maurice Johnston

Y is for no other than club captain George Young – winner of six League Championships, four Scottish Cups and two League Cups in the forties and early fifties. A true Rangers giant, 'Corky' (he always carried a champagne cork for luck) was also an 'Iron Curtain' defender (both at centre-half and right-back) who captained Scotland on no less than 48 occasions in 53 international appearances.

Z The final letter in the alphabet is also the final letter in the surname of Albertz. Last but not least, gone but not forgotten, the German midfielder scored one of the most stunning of all Old Firm goals when, in January 1997, his blistering thirty yard free-kick recorded a maximum speed of 79.8 miles per hour before hitting the back of the net. Later, on that highly charged day at Celtic Park in May 1999 when Rangers secured the Championship, it was Jorg Albertz who converted the crucial penalty just before half-time to give his side a 2-0 advantage.

Jorg Albertz

MISSING WORD QUIZ

FILL IN THE NAME OF THE MISSING RANGER FROM THIS SELECTION OF SEASON 2003/04 FOOTBALL HEADLINES. THE CLUE IS IN THE DATE!

1 '................. IN LIKE HARE TO ENSURE NO EARLY DEMISE FOR RANGERS' TITLE THOUGHTS' 24.11.03

2 '.................... VANQUISHES DUNDEE' 28.9.03

3 '..................... IN THE ARM FOR McLEISH' 18.1.04

4 'HONEYMOON IS OVER FOR ....' 6.2.04

5 '....................... RETURNS IN STYLE' 22.2.04

6 'DJORKAEFF:-....................... CAN SETTLE RANGERS WITH MERE PRESENCE' 7.3.04

7 'RANGERS CLING TO .... OF HOPE' 18.4.04

8 'RANGERS SAVOUR .... MAGIC' 2.5.04

9 'SCRIPT IS PERFECT FOR DEADLY ....' 11.5.04

10 'MY FUTURE LIES WITH RANGERS, DECLARES ....' 18.5.04

ANSWERS ON PAGE 61

1. Can you name the opponents when Rangers began their European campaign at Ibrox in August 2003?

2. Whose goal gave Rangers an early lead that night?

3. Who netted the crucial winner two weeks later in the return leg?

4. Who scored his first-ever Ibrox goal when Rangers won their opening Champions League group game against VfB Stuttgart?

5. Prior to this game, how many goals had the German side lost in their opening five Bundesliga matches?

6. In early October, whose goal against Panathinaikos in Greece stunned the hostile home crowd?

7. What had the scorer forgotten before kick-off?

8. The attendance for the Manchester United game in Glasgow was higher than the number of spectators at the Ibrox Old Firm clash earlier that month. True or false?

9. In the above game, his name was on the night's only goal and he cleared a Craig Moore header off the line. Name the Englishman.

10. Name the player who opened the scoring when Panathinaikos came to Govan in early December?

ANSWERS ON PAGE 61

STRIKING GOLD

WILLIE THORNTON

A gentleman both off and on the field, Ibrox immortal Willie Thornton (who was never booked or dismissed at any time in his entire playing career) was a truly inspirational centre-forward and the first post-war Ranger to break the 100 goal barrier. With skill and style in abundance, he was absolutely lethal in the air and a high percentage of his goals were headed home from both distance and close range.

After joining the club as an amateur at the age of sixteen in March 1936 (on £1 a week expenses), he made his first-team debut at outside-right against Partick Thistle at Firhill on 2 January 1937. Turning seventeen in the spring of that year, he then signed professional terms and was reminded that 'from now on you are the architect of your own fortune' by manager Bill Struth at the time. Thornton claimed his first goal against Celtic in the 3-0 league victory of September 1937 and, by the following season (1938/39), was established as a regular in the side that lifted the title. His personal tally in that league campaign was 23 goals.

Like many of his generation, the player 'lost' the best part of six years to the Second World War during which time he served with distinction and was subsequently awarded the Military Medal for gallantry in the Sicilian campaign.

Returning to Ibrox after the war, Thornton won another three championships in 1946/67 (18 goals in 25 games), 1948/49 (an incredible 23 goals in just 29 games) and 1949/50 (11 goals in 19 games), in addition to the Scottish Cup triumphs of 1948, 1949 and 1950. A staggering crowd of 143,570 saw his winner in the Scottish Cup semi-final clash with Hibernian in March 1948 on the road to the first of those three aforementioned silver days. The April Scottish Cup Final of 1950 was another memorable occasion as Willie came so close to establishing a milestone for the club. After netting twice in the Hampden meeting with East Fife, a third strike had been disallowed (for offside) thus denying him the honour of becoming the first-ever Ranger to score a hat-trick in the final. One honour he did claim however was to be part of the first team in Scotland to win the domestic treble of League Championship, Scottish Cup and League Cup when Rangers lifted all three trophies in Season 1948/49.

Voted Player of the Year in 1952, Willie Thornton retired two years later in 1954. Hardly surprising, given the pedigree of the man, he was still scoring right up until the end and hit seven goals in just eight games in his final season of 1953/54.

Willie used to tell a lovely story about his second encounter with the legendary Mr. Struth when, a few weeks after signing, he was chosen to play in a benefit match at Brockville for a Falkirk player. Prior to kick-off, the great man inspected Willie's boots and asked how much he was paid. After the youngster nervously confirmed £1 a week, the manager replied - 'Any boy who can polish his football boots like that deserves more than a £1 a week. From now on you will receive £2 a week.' The manager walked away before Willie had the chance to tell him that it was actually his mother who cleaned his boots.

Surrounded by his team-mates, Willie Thornton is congratulated by manager Bill Struth

Scottish League Championships (50)

1891, 1899, 1900, 1901, 1902, 1911, 1912, 1913, 1918, 1920, 1921,
1923, 1924, 1925, 1927, 1928, 1929, 1930, 1931, 1933, 1934, 1935,
1937, 1939, 1947, 1949, 1950, 1953, 1956, 1957, 1959, 1961, 1963,
1964, 1975, 1976, 1978, 1987, 1989, 1990, 1991, 1992, 1993, 1994,
1995, 1996, 1997, 1999, 2000, 2003.

Scottish Cups (31)

1894, 1897, 1898, 1903, 1928, 1930, 1932, 1934, 1935, 1936, 1948,
1949, 1950, 1953, 1960, 1962, 1963, 1964, 1966, 1973, 1976, 1978,
1979, 1981, 1992, 1993, 1996, 1999, 2000, 2002, 2003.

Scottish League Cups (23)

1946/47, 1948/49, 1960/61, 1961/62, 1963/64, 1964/65, 1970/71,
1975/76, 1977/78, 1978/79, 1981/82, 1983/84, 1984/85, 1986/87,
1987/88, 1988/89, 1990/91, 1992/93, 1993/94, 1996/97, 1998/99,
2001/02, 2002/03.

European Cup Winners' Cup

Winners 1972
Runners up 1961, 1967.

The Victory Cup 1946.

RANGERS AND THE SPL QUIZ SEASON 2003/04

1. Who scored Rangers first and last goals of the SPL season?

2. Name the player who claimed consecutive doubles in the September clashes with Hearts and Dundee.

3. From the start of the season until the end of December, only two defenders scored in the league. Who were the players in question?

4. Rangers scored more SPL goals than Celtic in August.
    True or false?

5. In the first half of last season, Rangers netted five times in only one league game. Who were the Ibrox opponents that day?

6. In January and early February last season, Rangers won three consecutive SPL games by the same 1-0 margin. Name their opponents.

7. Who scored the opener when Dunfermline were defeated 4-1 at Ibrox in late March?

8. Who created both goals when Partick Thistle lost 2-0 at Ibrox in April 2004?

9. He claimed his first double of the season against Dundee United at Tannadice in late April. Name the player.

10. Motherwell were beaten 4-0 at Ibrox in early May. How many other times did Rangers score four goals at home in league matches?

ANSWERS ON PAGE 61

QUIZ ANSWERS

THE MANAGERS QUIZ

1. Jock Wallace back in 1976.
2. Bill Struth, Scot Symon, Jock Wallace, Walter Smith, Dick Advocaat and, of course, Alex McLeish.
3. They won every competition that they were eligible to enter – League Championship, Scottish Cup, Glasgow Cup, Charity Cup, Reserve Championship and Reserve Cup - a world record, since unequalled.
4. Sampdoria.
5. Nine years.
6. Jock Wallace – 1972-78 and 1983-86.
7. With Rangers winning his two matches in charge, Thornton remains the only Ibrox manager in history with a 100% record!
8. Dundee United.
9. True.
10. John Greig.

RANGERS AND THE DOMESTIC CUPS QUIZ SEASON 2003/04

1. Forfar.
2. Christian Nerlinger.
3. St. Johnstone.
4. Egil Ostenstad.
5. False – it was Alan McGregor.
6. Michael Mols.
7. Four – one in the first-half and the three in the shoot-out.
8. Hibernian.
9. Shota Arveladze and Peter Lovenkrands.
10. Ronald de Boer.

HEADLINE NEWS

1. A hooligan runs onto the pitch and tries to attack Fernando Ricksen during the Pittodrie SPL clash with Aberdeen.
2. Stephen Hughes scores with some fifteen minutes remaining and the Aberdeen resistance is finally broken.
3. Panathinaikos snatch an equaliser right at the end of the Champions League encounter to deny Rangers an epic victory.
4. Christian Nerlinger's Ibrox goal means defeat for the lions of Livingston.
5. Brave Rangers come from behind to defeat VfB Stuttgart in the Champions League.
6. It was like the Rangers of old as Alex McLeish's side hit four past Dunfermline in the first 25 minutes of the game.
7. Stefan Klos is once again in superb form as Alex McLeish ends his Fir Park hoodoo with a close 1-0 victory over Motherwell.
8. With only twenty seconds of three injury-time minutes remaining, Stephen Hughes scores the winner at Easter Road against Hibernian.
9. Hearts keeper Craig Gordon defies Rangers time and time again in the 1-1 Tynecastle draw.
10. As rumours circulate regarding possible foreign signings, Scots Steven Thompson and Gavin Rae both score in the 2-0 win over Partick Thistle.

THE QUOTES QUIZ

1. Youngster Hamed Namouchi after his impressive debut in the Scottish Cup tie with Hibernian at Easter Road in January 2004.
2. Speaking in January 2004, Paoli Vanoli on life at Ibrox.
3. Manager Alex McLeish speaking about Stefan Klos in January 2004.
4. Ronald de Boer before heading for pastures new in Qatar.
5. Chris Burke speaking after his return from injury in March 2004.
6. Alex McLeish speaking about Marvin Andrews in April 2004.
7. Prior to arriving at Ibrox, 34-year-old Alex Rae confirms that his age is of no consequence.
8. Dado Prso on why he decided to join Rangers.
9. Marvin Andrews speaking about growing up in Trinidad.

MISSING WORD QUIZ

1. BURKE (Second half substitute Chris Burke is a major influence in the Ibrox victory over Aberdeen)
2. VANOLI (With a 1-1 draw looking likely, Paolo Vanoli's stunning 25 yard strike four minutes from time changed everything in the Ibrox clash with Dundee)
3. SHOTA (Motherwell are beaten 1-0 at Ibrox courtesy of Arveladze's late goal)
4. FRANK (In his second game since arriving from Turkey, Frank de Boer misses from the spot in the CIS Cup penalty shoot-out with Hibernian)
5. THOMPSON (Steven Thompson returns from long-term injury to score in the 3-0 victory over Hibernian at Ibrox)
6. BOUMSONG (French international Youri Djoekaeff speaking about Jean-Alain)
7. RAE (Midfielder Gavin Rae tops a great performance with Rangers' second in the 2-0 win over Partick Thistle)
8. BURKE (Chris Burke quite superb once again – this time in the 4-0 victory over Motherwell)
9. DADO (Dado Prso is absolutely delighted to be joining Rangers)
10. ARVELADZE (Despite interest from Ajax, Norwich and West Brom, Shota pledges his future to Rangers)

RANGERS IN EUROPE QUIZ SEASON 2003/04

1. FC Copenhagen.
2. Peter Lovenkrands.
3. Shota Arveladze.
4. Christian Nerlinger.
5. Not one.
6. Emerson.
7. His boots – they had been left on the team coach.
8. False – 48,730 as opposed to 49,825 for the Celtic game.
9. Phil Neville.
10. Michael Mols.

RANGERS AND THE SPL QUIZ SEASON 2003/04

1. Peter Lovenkrands and Ross McCormack.
2. Shota Arveladze.
3. Paolo Vanoli (v Dundee 27.9.03) and Michael Ball (v Dundee 28.12.03).
4. True – 15 as opposed to Celtic's 12.
5. Hibernian (5-2, 23.8.03).
6. Motherwell, Livingston and Partick Thistle.
7. Alan Hutton.
8. Alan Hutton.
9. Steven Thompson.
10. Four.